T0065682

The Language of Love

of

Love

JEREMIAH WHITE

WESTBOW
PRESS®
A DIVISION OF THOMAS NELSON
& ZONDERVAN

WestBow Press books may be ordered through booksellers or by contacting:

WestBow Press
A Division of Thomas Nelson & Zondervan
1663 Liberty Drive
Bloomington, IN 47403
www.westbowpress.com
844-714-3454

ISBN: 978-1-6642-9095-2 (sc)
ISBN: 978-1-6642-9096-9 (e)

Library of Congress Control Number: 2023901626

Print information available on the last page.

WestBow Press rev. date: 02/08/2023

Preface

God is always speaking. Jesus Himself stated, "My sheep hear my voice, and I know them, and they follow me" (John 10:27 KJV). God holds hidden secrets and divine mysteries that He wants to reveal to us. He has practical plans, strategies, and ideas that He desires for us to have for kingdom businesses, ministries, and our families. We need wisdom for raising our children, family relationships, finances, and building kingdom wealth. What if you could hear His voice and know practical next steps and strategies for the very problem that you are facing right now?

The issue for many of us is that we do not know how to discern when God is speaking. It is one thing to understand and be able to discern the meaning of scripture, but it is quite another to know how to hear God in real time when it comes to life choices. Imagine that your boss offered you a promotion that required relocation; would you make the right choice? Would you be able to hear from God, or would your decision be based upon how you feel? What if you were in a financial bind and in a time crunch to figure it out, would you know how to hear from God in real time to discover His plan of provision? God Himself tells us in Proverbs that we are to "lean not on our own understanding." Scripture also tells us that the "carnal mind is enmity against God" (Romans 8:7 NKJV). What does that mean? The carnal mind is a worldly perspective or "the way that seems right to men." Over the past three years, I have seen God move in ways that at first glance did not make sense in the natural yet turned out to be amazingly orchestrated opportunities for growth and provision. By being able to hear his voice and seek His input, He was able to lead me into the path that He chose for me and my family.

While editing this book, I lived in Florida and worked in a high-volume retail store. My income was mostly sales based, which meant that the busier we were, the more my commission checks grew. Even though I worked in a high-volume store and was very comfortable, God told my family that He wanted to move us back to Kansas. I was very excited for the prospect of a new beginning back home. Before moving, I asked the Lord if I was going to continue to work for the same company or if He was moving me elsewhere. The company that I worked for had just merged with another company, which opened up many opportunities. I was very excited to see what God was going to do financially. One night as I was sleeping, I had a dream that I was working for the company that my company had just merged with. I woke up knowing that God had answered my prayer. I was excited and even told my bosses that God had confirmed to me that I would be working for the other company that we merged with. In the period of a week, I found out that my district manager and regional manager were both quietly moved to other states. I had previously built relationships with them, and in the natural, it seemed that God would use them to land me in my new position. So I began to pray and thank God that He had the right place for me to work and minister. At work, shortly thereafter, a coworker told me that I needed to be more proactive about trying to find my own way into a high-traffic store. He felt that if I did not try to figure it out, I may end up without income. I felt a twinge of fear at the prospect that I could end up without a job, especially after such an expensive move across the country. After discussing things with my wife and current manager, I decided to leave the decision in God's hands and "lean not on my own understanding." In a short time, I was called by the recruiting office in Kansas. The only stores that needed staffing were with the company that we merged with.

It happened exactly according to my dream. Again, my faith was invigorated, knowing that God had my back and was leading.

So we moved to Kansas. Within a few days, I started working at my new store. The first day I entered the building, I saw a massive store with great potential. However, I found out that we were a low-traffic store. In the natural, it would seem that I had made a huge mistake. My income could potentially be dwindled to a third of what I normally made. This would have been frightening; however, I kept reminding myself that God was in control. He was leading the journey, and we could trust Him to provide for us.

A week later, many of our original stores around the area closed down. My store made the cut. Suddenly, the traffic from the other stores began to funnel into our store. Looking back, I realize that while we were slow, I was given time to learn the systems that we would use for their sales. Now, with a much higher-volume store, I was able to not only sell to the customer base that I was accustomed to, but I was also able to sell products to customers of the other company. God turned the circumstances around, but it took time and trust. This is one of a multitude of testimonies that you will read in this book. My hope is that you will see that we have a faithful God who has designed a path for each one of us. He wants to lead us in "paths of righteousness" where we will grow in our understanding and grow to become more like Him. He longs to take us on journeys that at first glance may not make sense with the natural or human perspective, but as we follow, they will lead us into the best place possible. The fruits of these decisions will be amazing. However, God wants to walk with us.

Doing what makes sense in the natural, trying to figure out our own way, may seem to pay off in the short term, but these both lead to disappointment. Why? Because as we face opposition, it causes us to doubt that we are in the right place. This leads to disappointment, disillusionment, and fear. But when we let God lead and follow His voice, we can rest knowing that He has every detail mapped out. This allows us to watch as God destroys our enemy beneath our feet. Mountains will crumble, and giants that stand in our way will fall. We are called, as Christians, to slay Goliaths. There are many things we are going to overcome in our lives if we partner with God. This is why we are to not lean on our own understanding or what would make sense to the logical mind. If we listen to our logic, to what makes sense to the natural way of thinking, we often miss God's opportunities to reveal His glory and power through us, and we settle with a lesser imitation. God may bless our choice, because He loves us, but we still miss out on many of the blessings that come with patience, trust, and obedience.

So if making decisions based on feelings or human knowledge does not reveal His plan, how can we know what to do? The short answer is that we must learn how to hear His voice. Since Jesus is the good shepherd and He leads us, it stands to reason that we need to allow Him to lead us. It also tells me that I need to learn how to hear His voice so that I can clearly follow His leading.

How does God communicate with us? Most of us cannot see Him with our natural eyes, which makes it more challenging to be led in the natural sense. Imagine with me, for a moment, that the Lord has something important to say to you. First, He tries speaking to you in the still, small voice, but because there are so many loud voices screaming at you, His voice gets drowned out. So he tries to speak to you in dreams. However, most Christians do not recognize that He is speaking, so you forget the dream. So then He decides that He is going to get creative (i.e., speaking to Moses in a burning bush). Scripture says, "The Lord himself goes before you and will be with you." God is outside of time. Scripture says that He has gone before us. I imagine that He walked the road that we would travel ahead of time. Because He knew what we would face, He planted treasures and messages for us to find, to help us along our journey. His help can look like billboards, the license plate on the car in front of you, or a timely song on the radio to the one trained to discern His voice. Jesus stated that His sheep do hear His voice. Since God is always speaking, we need to learn how to decipher what He is saying.

When we hear from God in real-life situations, it allows God to input His wisdom and His desires into the situation. I remember speaking to a young member of our worship team at church. I asked God what He wanted to say to the young man, and I heard that God was going to provide for him. Though I did not realize it at the time, he was in the process of moving to another state. He was under a great deal of stress because he did not know how he was going to provide for himself financially. The realization that God was going to provide for him brought him so much peace that he was in the right mindset for a divine encounter days later and was able to share the Lord with someone he met in a passing town. A few months later, he called to thank me and share how much the prophetic word meant to him. He asked if there was anything specific that he could pray about for us. As he was praying for me, I asked the Lord for another word for him. What God told me was so specific that I risked looking like a fool if I was wrong; but out of obedience, I told him what I heard. He was so caught off guard that he threw his phone. Through hearing God's voice, he received the answer to something that he had been asking for several months. The young man told me later that he knew that God had answered. Through that encounter, he received direction and wisdom that could only come from Jesus.

"My sheep hear My voice."

Jesus speaks to His people. Jesus said that His sheep (those who are being led by Him) do hear His voice. It is vital that we know that God wants to help us. He desires to invade our circumstances with power, love, wisdom, and creativity. God has an incredible plan for our lives. But how would we ever manage to discover His plans if He did not make a way to speak into our specific circumstances? It is vital that we not only believe that He wants to share His ideas with us but also know that we will hear and intercept His plan. Our Father does not withhold anything good from us. He is a good Father, which means that we can talk to Him anytime we desire to.

It is also essential to understand that the reason Jesus calls us sheep is because He knows that, just as sheep are helpless and rely upon their shepherd, we desperately need Him. He is telling us that we can trust Him. When we need to know what to do, we will hear His voice. As the good shepherd, He will help direct the lives of His sheep.

Disciples of Jesus understand their utter dependence upon Him. They want to fulfill His plans for their life. They desire to know Him more intimately and grow to become like Him. If you are the person who knows that you need Him and are passionate for Him to transform every aspect of your life, then this book is absolutely for you. He is speaking to you, and you will grow to discern it.

For the remainder of this book, I desire to help establish a grid of communication between you and the Father. I desire to help develop a telephone cable, so to speak, between you and God that will allow you to intercept His ideas, plans, thoughts, and confirmations for your life.

If you are open to hearing His voice, I believe that God is going to take you on an adventure with Him, which will ultimately lead to a new way for Him to speak with you.

At key points in each chapter, I am going to pray for you to receive impartations of new ways of hearing from God. Read these prayers and receive by thanking God for opening up these things to you. It is as simple as saying, "Yes, Jesus, I want to Hear from You clearly."

Introduction

To walk you through my journey of learning to hear His voice, I think it might be helpful to tell you a little bit about myself. My name is Jeremiah. I fell in love with Jesus and His Word as a young child. I grew up in a denominational church where I developed a foundation of biblical understanding. I knew God called me to preach the gospel from a young age. After high school, I attended a Baptist Bible seminary, where I met the love of my life, my sweetheart—Genger. For twenty years, I bounced back and forth between religion and rebellion. I struggled with pornography, which eventually led me to leave the marriage covenant in pursuit of happiness. After thirteen years of hell and a broken home, Jesus came to my rescue. After an encounter with Jesus, I was set completely free and on fire for Him and His kingdom. A year or so into my conversion experience, this journey began.

As a result of learning to hear God's voice, He brought restoration to my marriage, finances, credit score, children's schooling, and family relationships. Genger and I are happier than we have ever been. We have two beautiful children who know their identity and walk by hearing God's voice. After returning home from our two-year excursion with the Lord, currently we live in Kansas.

My wife and I spent most of our married life in Kansas. In the spring of 2018, God told my family to pack our van with as much as we could carry and drive to Atlanta, Georgia. Though we did not know anyone there, we obeyed. We had no idea what we were doing, nor did we understand the faith required of us as we stepped into Georgia. Our faith journey would have been much more stressful had we not first learned how to accurately hear His voice. Discerning His will and hearing His voice allowed us to move confidently, despite how things appeared at the moment, even when others told us we were making a mistake. My goal is to help you establish the same type of communication with God that will allow you to accurately hear His voice and be able to move as He opens doors for you. He has amazing plans for all of us that require us to be able to discern where He is leading. The old ways of using feelings or human reasoning as our guides must end if we are to embark on the path that leads to our destinies.

I pray you enjoy this book and know that God is drawing you into a deeper relationship with Him.

One

I See You, and I Love You

I was in a spiritual place of deep hunger for God, in a season where I was in His presence for hours per day, experiencing miraculous healing miracles. My faith was expanding rapidly. During this time, while ministering to a neighbor in our apartment complex, the Lord introduced me to a man named Sean. Sean is an intense and zealous man, most known for his full gray beard and his passion for Jesus.

Sean helped open up a place for my neighbor to live while he was working on his marriage and working through alcohol addiction. After meeting up and discussing our relationship with Jesus, Sean and I instantly became friends. After talking on the phone a few times, our friendship blossomed until we talked for hours per day.

One day as we were hanging out, Sean told me that God spoke to Him in "numbers." I had no idea what this was, but the concept was intriguing. As we would go to grocery stores praying for people, sequences of numbers would catch his attention. He would point it out and chuckle, as if he had received an inside joke from the Lord.

I remember asking God to speak to me in ways He had never spoken to me before. Until then, God had spoken to me through dreams, song lyrics, and scripture, but if there were other ways of hearing from Him, I wanted in. One day, God granted me my desire. I was going about my day when my eyes were drawn to my phone.

The time display showed the number 111. I didn't think much about it at the time. A little while later, I went into a gas station to refill gasoline. As I picked up the receipt, I noticed 111 in sequence on the ticket. I started to take notice. While driving to take my wife to work, a car pulled in front of me. Can you guess what numbers were on the license plate? It became apparent that it wasn't a coincidence. I began to wonder if God was trying to tell me something. And if so, what would He be saying to me? I asked the Lord what it meant. I heard the words, "I see you, and I love you." That was a beautiful thought, but I wanted confirmation. Though I had a definition for the number, I had no idea why I saw it or from where it came.

I remember one particular day, months later, the enemy was bombarding me with lies. I was tired and worn out from the temptation. I felt like I had blown it. My family was days away from moving, and I was not yet sure where God was sending us. That night, I experienced a full assault from the enemy that seemed to last for hours. Afterward, it left me feeling defeated. I didn't know why, but the clock grabbed my attention. I saw the number 111. I suddenly remembered the words "I see you and love you." Wow, what a sense of love washed over me. The anxiety and torment left, and peace flooded the room as I remembered at that moment that God saw me. He knew what I was going through. Hope filled my soul. My focus shifted from my circumstances back to Christ. God loved me despite what I perceived as failure. He had not changed His mind about me. This encounter completely changed my perspective and my attitude.

Since then, I have seen the number quite frequently. For years, I have seen 111 while experiencing victories, such as seeing someone get healed when I am doing nothing at all, and especially during periods of hardship and growth. The truth remains the same. Father God loves us and is proud of His children. Though I now had a basic concept of what it meant, I still did not have a scriptural basis for why I saw the number. I asked God to tell me why I saw this and to give me a scripture.

One day, while Sean and I were chatting, out of nowhere, he said, "Yeah, it's just like Mark 1:11 (KJV) says, 'This is my beloved Son, in whom I am well pleased.'" I don't think I heard anything else that Sean said because, in an instant, I understood why I saw 111. I knew that God was confirming what 111 meant. He had given me scripture to back it up. It was no longer a mystical number. God was speaking to me from a particular scripture that held the key I needed at that moment. I needed to remember that God saw me as His son, and He was pleased with me. I felt so much joy and peace knowing God was speaking to me. I felt resolute that He had invited me into a deeper conversation with Him.

It was the fall of 2018 in Atlanta. My family lived in the back of a ministry that fed people experiencing homelessness. I was working for a temp agency at the time for a minimal wage. The outreach where we were staying asked my wife, Genger, to speak at a gala on the topic of homelessness in one of the most luxurious golf clubs in the city. Due to a mix-up with our vehicle payment, the bank repossessed our only vehicle—in view of a group of celebrities who were shooting a popular film.

Fear and anxiety became my constant companion for some time. As a result of the repossession, I would walk long distances to the train station and then take a bus, which got me within a mile of the job site. From there, I would walk the rest of the way to work. I was making very little money while working sixty hours a week. I was exhausted and couldn't help but wonder if I had somehow missed God's best for our family.

One day as I was walking to the train station, my eyes were drawn to a parking meter. There on the side were the numbers 111 in big white letters. Though it was a long, arduous walk, and it was very early in the morning, it brought me so much peace to remember that Father loved me and was proud of my hard work. I felt His pleasure and knew He saw me and was proud of me. I knew that He was with us.

A few months prior, we were almost entirely out of gas. My wife and I were waiting for interviews for the jobs we had applied for. We were standing in faith and believing God would provide gas and food. A good friend messaged me through a series of circumstances and asked if we were okay. I shared what we needed God to provide for us. He called me back and told me to meet him. He collected money from some friends and brought it to us. As we pulled into the gas station, running on fumes, we couldn't help but notice in big white numbers in front of the building the address of 111.

Whenever I see the number 111, I remember Mark 1:11. I remember that, like Christ, I am His beloved son, and He is pleased with me. It reminds me that I am "be-loved," not "do-loved." I am responsible for receiving His love and not trying to earn it. His love hinges not upon my work but on who He is and His finished work. As Jesus hung upon the cross, His wide-open arms screamed love and peace for us. "But God demonstrates (proves) His own love toward us, in that while we were yet sinners (or living in sin), Christ died for us" (Romans 5:8 NASB). He is love! And from that perspective, He is proud of me. He is proud of the fact that I am His son. He is proud of my desire to follow Him, which is surprising because He is the one who placed that desire within me. All things are from Him and flow through us back to Him.

The truth is that He loves you as well. "God is no respecter of persons" (Acts 10:34 KJV). God does not pick favorites. God would never have chosen me if He decided who His sons would be based on performance. It seems that God chooses the weak and foolish, lowly and despised. Paul put it this way: "But God hath chosen the foolish things of the world to confound the wise; and God hath chosen the weak things of the world to confound the things which are mighty. And base (lowly) things of the world, and things which are despised, hath God chosen, yea, and things which are not, to bring to naught things that are: that no flesh should glory in his presence" (1 Cor. 1:27–29 KJV). God chose Israel, one of the tiniest and weakest nations, to be His chosen people. God chose Gideon, a soft and insecure man, to save His people. God has chosen you. Do you ever feel like you are too far gone? Do you wonder if God even knows who you are? You are a candidate for His grace and glory. He wants to make you into someone so captivating that it causes the world to ask, "Who are you?"

God has prepared a way for all people to become His children and, therefore, right with God. If you have accepted Christ, Jesus has already made you right with God. You are now a member of the beloved family of God. God loves you because of who you are. You are His son or daughter, and He is pleased with you. He is pleased that you are part of His family. He is ecstatic that you chose to say yes to Him. Since you are His, rest assured that He will begin to talk to you in more and more creative ways.

If you are reading this book and have never accepted Jesus, I want to introduce Him to you. Jesus is God's Son. From the beginning, God designed grandiose plans and purposes for each of us. God created us in His image, but sin mangled and twisted our lives so much that they no longer resembled His design. As a result, we have all experienced death, pain, sickness, disease, and torment. But life was not supposed to be this way. So God decided that one day He would send His Son. Jesus's destiny was to take on a physical body, come to Earth, live the perfect, sinless life, and curse sin by hanging on a tree. As a result, sin lost its power; God would remove our sin, forgive us completely, and restore everything in our lives, bringing us back to the way God intended for us in the garden. Jesus did not die merely to take you to heaven when you die; He died to remove your sin, pain, sickness, and disease. How do I know this? Jesus said that it is His will for all to be saved. *Saved* is the Greek word *sozo*, which means saved, healed, delivered, made well, and prospered.

While traveling to work one day, Jesus told me to look at the gospels. When the woman who had the issue of blood determined that if she could touch the hem of His garment, she would be healed, do you remember what she did? She made her way through the crowd and touched His robe. Scripture says that she was made whole. If you look at the word *whole*, it is the same word as sozo. Almost every time the words *saved, healed, made whole,* or *delivered* are found in the New Testament, they all point to the same thing. Jesus saved them. He healed their diseases. He delivered them from demons. He desires everyone would be sozo.

All that it takes from you is a yes. If you admit that you have sinned and are willing to die to your old life, He will come and make all things new for you. He will give you a new life.

In the same way God used my friend Sean to open new lines of communication with me and show me what was possible, He will do the same for you. As you begin to see numbers, I pray that you will start to ask the Lord what they mean and keep seeking wisdom. His Word says that His Spirit searches the deep things of God and has revealed them unto us (1 Cor. 2:10). If we ask for discernment in faith, He will give it freely to us.

After sharing these testimonies with others, I have had several tell me that they began to see 111 as well. I believe that as you read the rest of this book, Father will open these truths up to you, giving you unique communication methods to share with Him so that you can share them with others.

Note the focus is to be on Jesus. I am not advocating a new formula or method for getting answers. We must not chase numbers; instead, we ask Him questions and allow Him to answer. Numbers give God a new way to answer us in the natural.

The more we see and meditate on scripture, the more robust our foundation will be. The more truth we know and apply from scripture, the more we will see and hear God's responses. Everything comes down to having a relationship with Christ and dependence upon Him. Spend time with Him and grow in Him, and you will find that He will expand your understanding and wisdom. He wants to build a foundation of truth in us that is laid solidly upon His Word.

At the end of each chapter, I will pray for you to receive the impartation of new ways of hearing from God. Read these prayers aloud and receive them by thanking God for opening these things up to you.

> *Father, I thank You for my brothers and sisters in Christ. I thank You for always speaking to us. I thank You that You desire intimacy with us and a relationship more than anything else. I honor You for sharing these things with me, and I impart these treasures of wisdom to them in Jesus's name! Speak to them in ways that You never have before. I ask that You fill them with the Spirit of wisdom and revelation in the knowledge of You. Thank You for allowing me to share these things and help teach Your bride to hear Your voice in Jesus's name. Amen.*

Now it's your turn:

> *Father, I want to get to know You more. I desire to hear Your voice and for You to speak to me in ways You never have before. I trust You that You will lead me. I ask that You give me Your wisdom and the confidence to know that I hear Your voice and will follow You. Thank You, Father, for speaking to me however You choose. In Jesus's name, amen.*

Two

I See You, and I Will Provide

Shortly after I started seeing the number 111, I began to notice 1111. I now understood that God was speaking to me, and my hunger grew to know what He was telling me. I asked the Lord what it meant. I heard, "I see you, and I will provide."

My friend Sean, who I have enjoyed watching the Lord grow in his gifting and love for the Lord, said one day, "It's just like Luke 11:11 (NASB) says, 'If a son asks for bread from any father among you, will He give him a stone? Or if he asks for a fish, will He give him a serpent instead of a fish?'" Again, I heard the Father's voice through my friend and knew he was confirming what God had been speaking to me.

During this season, we were experiencing a tremendous lack in the natural realm. We had promises and prophetic words of abundance and favor, yet all we could see was scarcity. Father revealed to me that He saw us and knew what we needed. In the same way that I would do whatever it takes to meet my children's needs, my ability and desire paled in comparison to His. He desires to see us step into the destiny and provision He has prepared for us. We must learn to stand and find rest in the promise even when the manifestation has not yet come. Thus the purpose of 1111 for us.

A couple of years later, God asked my family of four to leave everything behind and follow Him from Kansas City to Atlanta. After we arrived, Genger and I applied for and were waiting to hear back from our job interviews. Because it took longer than we anticipated, we depleted all of our savings. To make matters worse, every morning, we had to leave the outreach by seven o'clock before the staff showed up, and we couldn't come back until the staff left for the day. The extra driving proved challenging, as we had no income for gas or food and nowhere to go. One day as we were on our way to the public library, my ten-year-old daughter pointed out a billboard with the number 1111. Through her, God reminded us that He was going to provide. We were all filled with hope and courage as we remembered what His Word says. The sign was more than a generic word about provision. We knew that God was going to provide for us in real time. It reminded us of His faithfulness. Since our heavenly Father is good, He will give us what we need. Papa knows what we ask him for before we even pray. He is the God who provides.

He kept His promise to us. God supernaturally provided food and gas. As we prayed about how God wanted to provide, He reminded us of a washer and dryer set we no longer needed in Kansas. We messaged my sister and asked if she would be willing to post it for sale. Within a short time, someone offered the exact amount that we needed. A few hours later, she sold the set and transferred the money to us. We drove into the gas station and ran out of gas as we pulled in. My family cheered God on as we coasted into the pump. Other people at the pump recognized what was happening and began cheering and praising God! It was such a beautiful picture of the goodness and love of God. Not only were we able to get gas and food, but we also made it to church on time. Father God provided for us just like He had told us through the billboard. He was speaking, and it motivated us to keep going.

Here are some things to ask yourself:

- Have you seen any specific series of numbers regularly? Have you ever wondered if God was speaking to you?

- Do you pay attention to the things around you and how God speaks?
- When you start seeing 111 or 1111, will you recognize that Father has something to say to you?
- Are you willing to allow God to create an open line of communication where He can speak into the natural realm through different ways to talk to you and lead you to scripture for your answers?

Ask the Holy Spirit to reveal ways He has been speaking so you can partner with Him. You do not have to "hear" anything immediately. Give him time, and He will show you.

> *Father, I thank You for opening up new ways of communication with Your bride. I thank You that You will open our eyes to see how You speak to us. Draw us into a greater level of mystery and wonder. Speak "now" words to us that correspond to real-life situations. Thank You for speaking to us in new ways. In Jesus's name! Amen.*

Three

Come and Spend Time with Me

"Call unto me, and I will answer you and show you
great and mighty things which you do not know."
—Jeremiah 33:3 (NKJV)

When I first started seeing numbers, another number I began
to see was 333. I had no idea what it meant. I had heard
from someone else that it meant unity, which kind of made sense
because the number three stands for the Trinity, which is, of course,
the Father, Son, and Holy Spirit. But I wondered why it would not
be just three. Why was it 333? This number puzzled me for a while.

One evening at church, a pastor prophesied that I was going to
be having an encounter with the Lord and that the scripture for the
season that I was in was Jeremiah 33:3. I realized then that 333 was
a call to come and be intimate with Him because He had things to
share with me. He has promised that if we come to Him, He will
share ideas with us, secrets that we have never seen or heard before.

When I see 333 now, I know there's something the Lord wants
to discuss with me. It's a call to get away from the hustle and bustle
and be silent before Him.

There is nothing more fulfilling in life than getting away to be
with Him. It was during time alone with God that He miraculously

opened a position for me at one of my favorite companies. I had previously applied to three different stores for the same job and was rejected for all three. I even received an email that stated that I was not what they were looking for. One night while asking God where I was supposed to work, He told me that there was one position that He had been saving for me. I applied and was offered the job.

In March 2020, as I was driving home from work, my wife and I were both drawn to the numbers 333 on a billboard. Out of habit, we asked God what He wanted to tell us. God told me that I would indeed be finished with this book by a certain date. At the same time, He told my wife that He wanted her to fast for a couple of days. I love how God is interested in communicating with each of us individually. God may speak to me in one way and may choose to speak with you in another way. God may give me a specific scripture and truth for a set of numbers and then give you a different verse. This is why it is essential that you seek your revelation through intimacy with God.

God has so much to say. He wants to speak into our lives. What would change if we asked Him and invited Him into every situation of life? What would happen if we brought every challenge and struggle before Him? Every time we see the number 333, let's commit to taking time to be alone with Him.

Here are some things to consider:

- How often do you rest in God's presence and allow Him to talk to you?
- How much of your quiet time do you spend talking and asking for things without giving Him a chance to speak?
- God knows that there is knowledge and wisdom that you need right now. Would it be helpful to have a way for Him to call you away to be with Him?
- When you see 333, will you remember Jeremiah 33:3 and call upon Him?

Father, we thank You that You desire a relationship with us. Thank You that we hear Your voice and that we can do what we see the Father doing. As we are calling out for You, give us wisdom and revelation. Open our eyes to see and ears to hear. I ask right now that You keep connecting the lines of communication between You and Your bride. Show us more of Your Word and remind us of Your scriptures. Teach us to be in Your Word and students of Your Word, in Jesus's name. I also ask that You remove all fear of Your new-to-us ways of speaking and instead fill us with awe and wonder. I ask that You confirm to everyone reading this book that You are indeed behind it. Thank You, Father, as I trust You.

Four

Sign or Confirmation

M y wife and I sat at a friend's house in Buford, Georgia, and explained how we were not sure where we were supposed to move. The landlord at our current home had decided unexpectedly to evict our family. Although we were current on our rent payments, he ran into financial struggles. He felt that it was the best time to sell. As a family, we began praying for Father to reveal to us where we were supposed to go next. That night, as I explained where we were in the process, I felt the Holy Spirit say that we were to all pray together. As my friend Daniel prayed, I heard we were moving to Florida. Previously, a door had opened in Navarre Beach, Florida, for us with the deposit paid, but we weren't sure it was the right place or time. After all, the Lord had audibly told me to move to Georgia (which is rare for me to hear that way), and we did not want to step out of His plan. That night, after hearing clearly, I asked the Lord to confirm if we were to go. As we drove home, my wife said, "Hey, look at that billboard." As I looked up, I saw the numbers 444 and 1111. I instantly heard that He was confirming to me that we were going to move to Florida and that He would provide for us on the way. A few minutes later, we saw the same billboard. After we arrived home, my wife was still not convinced. She asked the Lord to confirm to her that we were moving. She looked down at her phone, and the time was 4:44.

The number 444 was a challenge for me for several years. The biggest question that remained in my mind was "Where is this in scripture?" I asked the Lord, and I heard, "Sign or confirmation." But like any Berean, I want to see it in scripture. I want to know that I am hearing Him clearly and then will follow His leading. One day after asking the Lord where I could find this in scripture, He took me to Isaiah 44:4. God was reminding the children of Israel of His covenant with them. He told them that because they were His chosen people, that was how He would fulfill or confirm His covenant with them. The Father would take their dry places, fill them with water, bless them, and pour His Spirit upon their children. He gave a sign or confirmation of His love and covenant with them.

Since then, God has confirmed many things to me, using Isaiah 44:4 as a reference to reveal His love and promises. He loves to prove and show the world that we are His.

While at work one day, I was contemplating the offer by a good friend of the family to come down to Navarre Beach in Florida and minister with them. It sounded like a great time, but I knew that our income was minimal. I had to ensure that God was in it and that He would fund it. Financially, we did not have the resources to make the trip. However, whenever we are around the Gilyeat family, we are drawn into a deeper walk with the Lord. We have seen so many radical encounters of healing, deliverance, and prophetic words as we all minister everywhere we go. I asked the Lord if He wanted us to go. I instantly heard the song lyrics, "I love to feel the sand underneath my feet with the tropical sun shining down." As I looked up, on the windshield of the car nearest me was a vendor tag that contained the number 444. Then I saw another vehicle. There again was the number 444.

We went and had radical times of worship, growth, and ministry. We saw several people get healed; one lady was filled with the Spirit and encountered the love of the Father. Our friends blessed us with many brand-new kitchen utensils, bedding sheets, and miscellaneous items for our new apartment. We knew this was the beginning of our provision for the next season. God confirmed through Isaiah 44:4 that He was blessing us as a sign of His covenant with us.

One day when I walked out of Walmart in Fayetteville, Georgia, I suddenly had a pounding headache. I had walked with the Lord long enough to recognize a word of knowledge. My family and several friends would often go on scavenger hunts and pray for people to be healed in public, often based on words of knowledge about what types of illnesses we would see. For those who have never experienced this, a "word of knowledge" is when the Holy Spirit shares something with you that you would not know through any natural means. God was showing me that someone close by was having migraines. I looked around and began asking the Lord who He wanted me to pray for. I saw a young lady walking through the entrance as I walked out of the exit, but there was no way that I could reach her fast enough to pray for her. I sensed that it wasn't her, so I kept walking ahead. Then I saw two younger ladies, possibly in their early twenties. *I wonder if it is one of these ladies*, I thought. As I looked in their direction, my eyes were drawn to the car right next to them. Guess what numbers were on the license plate? You guessed it, 444. I then knew God was giving me the answer so I could minister to them. I walked up and asked if one of them was having migraines. One of the two young ladies said she occasionally got migraines. She let me pray for her. It is incredible to see how God speaks and confirms things to us that we would have no other way to know. I would have had no idea who to pray over. What would have happened if God had not confirmed to me that it was one of the two young ladies? I could have missed out and walked back inside, but the girl might have never had an encounter with the Father's heart for her.

One of the most impactful testimonies of confirmation came a couple of weeks ago. My sister's daughter came to her and asked if she could spend the night at her friend's house. Typically, she would let her daughter go since she knew the mother. However, she looked up, only to see the number 666 on her phone. Because the Lord had trained her to hear His voice, she knew the enemy was up to something. Suddenly her eyes were drawn to 444 on the clock. With more resolve, my sister probed about who would be over at the house that evening. After some probing, she discovered that the girl's mother was working that night. Both young girls would be left alone with the mother's new boyfriend, who my sister did not know at all. By this point, she knew that the Lord had alerted her that the enemy had planned something so she could avoid it, and her daughter stayed safely at home. Had it not been for the line of communication she developed with God, my niece may have had a much different outcome.

Another time, my nephew wanted to go to his youth camp. His parents did not have the funds to go because it was a costly trip. My nephew reached out to the youth pastor to find out if they had any scholarships available. The pastor told him it was unlikely, but he would check and see. My son was talking to my nephew on the phone as he was sharing these things. My son and wife thanked God that he would be able to go and prayed for heaven to move for him. Instantly, my nephew said, "I just saw four-four-four. I know that I am going to be able to go."

On the night before they were to leave, my sister began to get nervous that he might not be able to go. Even though they had not heard back, my nephew believed that he had heard from God and was going. That night, the phone rang. It was the youth pastor. Last minute, someone could not go on the trip but had already paid. My nephew was able to go without paying anything!

Shortly after writing this chapter, my family packed our belongings in our Penske truck. We wanted to make a pit stop to spend time with some Spirit-filled friends before we moved to our new home in Navarre Beach. On the way, my daughter looked up and said, "Hey, Dad, look." We saw 666 on a sign as we drove in.

I felt no fear at the prospect that the enemy was looking to steal, kill, and destroy, but the previous night, I had a dream that I was to put a padlock on the back of our Penske truck before we moved. I wasn't exactly sure what that meant, but I knew that Papa would let me know. I filed the 666 in my mind, and a few moments later, we pulled into our friends' place.

We talked about God, the Holy Spirit, family, and life. Nearing the end of the trip, my friend asked me if I would meet him in his office for a few moments. I sensed that something was up but gladly proceeded. Once inside the office, my friend told me that he had heard that we were not to move to Florida. He told me he would be disobedient to God if he did not tell me. He mentioned that things were going to be very hard in our new place because we were stepping outside God's will. I knew that our friends loved us dearly. I knew that they wanted what was best for us. I do not doubt that he hears clearly from the Lord. But I knew what Father had spoken to me in many different ways. The 444 1111 confirmation, as well as God's voice, had confirmed to me that Papa wanted for us to go. I thanked him and went to a quiet place where I could speak with the Lord about what my friend had told me. The Lord once again confirmed to me that we were to go.

I realized just how much of a blessing it is to know for sure that you hear clearly from Father God. Had the Lord not developed a line of communication for me for several years, I might have moved away from His plan. It is crucial that we come to the place spiritually where we know His voice. My prayer is that Father will connect the dots for you. I pray that you will be able to discern that He is speaking to you.

> *I thank You, Papa, that You will confirm many things for my brothers and sisters, so they will know what Your will is for their lives. Thank You for Your signs and confirmations.*

God is always speaking. He wants to be part of everything that we do. Papa wants to help us in every way. He doesn't want us to do things for Him. God has called us to have dominion, to reign as kings and queens. However, He desires to cocreate with us.

What would it be like if God was able to communicate with you at work about which client to pursue? What if God could help confirm to you which stock to buy? Would it be helpful to know beforehand if a car was a lemon or if it would be reliable? What if God could tell you which answer was correct on the test (when you have studied but are unsure which to pick)? Can you see how numbers can give us a two-way dialogue with God?

God will speak to you in these ways. If you desire Him to open up these ways of communication with you, then it's as simple as asking Him in childlike faith. His Word says, "What we ask, believing, we will receive." Luke 11:11 again states that when we ask Him for good things, He will not give us anything fake or anything that will harm us. He is a good, good Father. God made us to have a relationship with us. He wants a two-way, open dialogue. While numbers are not the only way He speaks, they are one of the ways He can surprise, inform, and confirm things to us.

Father, I thank You that You are always speaking. I thank You that You would open up our eyes to see all of the ways that You are communicating with us. I also impart to them the gift of communication through numbers, in the name of Jesus!

Five

Buckle Up and Get Ready

E arly on in my journey of learning to hear the voice of the Lord, I saw the number 222. I asked the Lord what this meant. I heard *"Buckle up* and get ready," emphasizing *buckle up* (into Him). I saw this number for a while before my family left to come to Atlanta. Even after we moved to Georgia, I saw the number 222 frequently. One day, as I spent time with the Lord, He revealed that it wasn't about the "going." He told me that I needed to learn to buckle up into Him. I needed to be trained to abide in Him. I needed to keep myself in His Word. I needed to stay in union with Him. I needed to learn to stand upon His Word and securely attach myself to the truth so that I wouldn't fall.

One night at the outreach where we were staying, I encountered an angel. The angel had the face of what I can best describe as a hawk. He told me, "I didn't know how to use my sword yet." At first, I thought maybe it was a demon trying to discourage me. After I put my pride in check, I asked God what this meant. I did not hear anything immediately, but a short time after the encounter, I listened to the *Final Quest* audiobook by Rick Joyner. It was there that God revealed the answer to me. In *Final Quest*, the main character sees the mountain of the Lord. Soldiers were standing guard along various parts of the mountain. As they climbed higher, vultures would vomit and excrete filth all over the Lord's army. One soldier, through wisdom, saw several soldiers lose their balance and fall over the ledge, get wounded, and then be carried off by the enemy hordes. So he decided to stick his "sword" into the ground and tie a rope around it. This decision allowed him to stay securely attached and not fall. He learned to stand firmly upon the Word of God and secure (buckle) himself to Christ (the Word.) This way, no matter how high he went in gifting, calling, talent, or influence, he was securely buckled up into Christ. While the journey of learning to stand upon God's promises and His Word is ongoing, this proved to be very helpful as we navigated staying in faith through all of the testings of homelessness, poverty, and hard labor. Fear was crippling, but we kept standing on the truths of scripture to give us hope. Truth kept us from giving up and returning to our previous life.

Ephesians 2:22 says, "And in him or (in union with Him) you too are being built together into a dwelling for God's Spirit." God is building his church into the Temple of the Holy Spirit, but it requires us to stay in Him (be buckled up into Him). Get ready for whatever comes your way by staying close to Him. Keep yourself grounded in His Word and His love for you. Buckle up into Him!

Here are some things to consider:

- Are you getting into God's Word daily and asking Him what He wants to show you?
- Do you know what it means to attach yourself securely to the Word so that you do not succumb to the enemy's temptation? What does the concept of a seat belt show you about being buckled up into Him?
- God wants to teach you who you are and how to use the Word of God to stand.

Father, I thank You for teaching Your bride how to properly use the sword (Word of God). Teach us what it means to stay buckled up into You and be ready to become, do, and go wherever You call us. Thank You for speaking to us, Father. We ask for more wisdom to hear Your voice. I thank You that You would show us what we need to be more effective in Your kingdom.

Six

The Mystery Revealed

I love mysteries. From the time I was young, I enjoyed reading adventure books like *The Hardy Boys*. In a good mystery, you stay in suspense until the right moment, when the writer reveals the plot. Proverbs 25:2 says, "It is the glory of God to conceal a matter, but the glory of kings is to search out a matter." Do you know that there are mysteries that He has hidden in plain sight for you to find?

If you are the one who loves mysteries and enjoys the awe and wonder of God, I want to take you on a journey with me. While I am aware that this sounds incredible, it is absolutely true. I have been processing this encounter for several months and will likely be receiving revelations for years to come.

It all started as soon as my family obeyed the Lord and left Kansas City. I had been seeing a red A (reminded me of the Atlanta Braves emblem) for several months in different ways, but I wasn't sure what it meant. After several months of living with family, they told us we needed to move out within two weeks. Two nights before we were to leave, I woke up from a dream and heard clearly, "I want you to load up your van and take your family to Atlanta, Georgia." Though we had only fifty-four dollars in our wallet, we packed up and prepared to leave. Before we left Kansas, God showed up, blessed us with over $770, and again confirmed that we were heading to Georgia. Though we didn't exactly know where we were going, Father led us. We stepped out on faith and trusted the Lord to work all things out for us. Once we arrived in Georgia, I began to see the number 808. I would see it on license plates in front of us, on the clock, on billboards, and on phone numbers. I knew God was speaking, so I asked what it meant. All I could hear was silence from Father. I started seeing the number every single day, which intrigued me. Then I started seeing 808 multiple times a day. I began to pay attention when I saw it to see if there were any hints about what it meant. I couldn't see any rhyme or reason.

One day, as I spent time with Father, I was given the impression that 808 was a mystery that He was inviting me into, which was exciting.

My family of four was living in what we called a one-room mansion. We lived there and saved money for about six months. The day came when the outreach gave us two days to leave. We had been saving money, and a place opened up to rent closer to our church, but I had not heard from Father whether or not we were heading in that direction. I was stressed. I went into our dorm room and began to cry out to God. "Why am I not hearing from You? Why did You bring us out here, and now we are being asked to leave?" God interrupted my complaining with a knock on the door. One of the pastors at the outreach asked if I would be willing to preach the evening service. Before I had time to think about it, I accepted. He thanked me and walked away. At that moment, I realized I did not have a message prepared. It had been several years since I had preached a sermon. I asked forgiveness for complaining and told the Lord that I realized He must have something to say. I gave Him my mouth, received what He wanted me to preach, and obeyed. That night, the Holy Spirit showed up powerfully. The group of people was tranquil and attentive as I revealed the Father's heart for them.

At the end of the message, a man in rags approached me and asked if I would be willing to sit with him for a moment. I started to ask Papa what He wanted to do with him. I instantly began to ask God for words for healing or prophetic for him. I heard nothing. As the man reached out to shake my hand, I felt as if I was ushered into the presence of God. I remember thinking, *Who is this?* My thoughts were interrupted by his voice, "My name is Abraham. I have a similar testimony as you." His language was very poetic and intellectual. As I listened to him speak, it reminded me of a King James Bible type of English. He told me things are not as they appear and kept mentioning the word *visitation*. It is what followed that blew me away. Abraham began to answer every question I had been asking the Lord. It was as if the Father handed him a notecard with all of my complaints. He began to answer them in order. Once this mysterious man finished prophesying hope into my future, Abraham noticed my daughter. He told me he needed to sit down with her and asked if it was okay. I motioned for my young daughter to come over as I introduced her to Abraham.

Abraham began to tell her things that she needed to hear. He answered complaints that she had been telling us, such as "You don't understand me." He shared with her that we loved her and were the only ones who truly understood her. He told her that she needed to ensure that she kept no secrets from us. Lastly, he said to her, "Your parents and I will always be with you." With that, he got up and left.

I couldn't sleep that night as I lay in bed thinking about what had just happened. Out of all the ways God could have answered me, He sent a messenger. I knew that I had just had a visitation from heaven. It wasn't until later that night, as I asked God what had happened, that the Lord revealed the mystery.

I was chatting with my sister about what had happened, and somehow the conversation came up about 808. Suddenly she said, "Woah." She found a website about Hebrew letters and the numbers that relate to each. There is a mathematical function for every Hebrew letter. Written on the website was the number 808, which means Abraham, the way or faith. Suddenly I knew what 808 meant. God was pointing me to the day that I would meet with Abraham.

He also pointed out that I needed to *believe* and have *faith* even when I could not see the answer with my eyes.

The next day, I heard where we were moving, and it became a fantastic time of rest and provision. From then on, when I saw 808, I heard the lyrics "Don't stop believing …" When I struggle in faith or am wavering on a promise He has given me, God shows me 808. It reminds me of the words that Abraham spoke into my life. It reminds me that we walk by faith and not by sight.

> *Father, I thank You that there is a great grace here to empower us to walk out everything You have called us to walk. I thank You for greater faith, for all of my brothers and sisters, to walk by faith and not by sight. Give us mysteries and the privilege of seeking out the matter. Thank You that Your Holy Spirit draws the deep things of God and reveals them to us. Thank You for Your Spirit of Revelation and Wisdom in the knowledge of You.*

Here are some thoughts to consider:

- Am I walking by faith or by sight?
- In what areas can I surrender to God's plan even when it may not make sense in the natural?
- Have I seen the number 808?
- Am I open to encounters from God to help guide my path? Are my eyes opened to see what God is doing that may go far beyond human wisdom or understanding?

> *Lord, open their eyes to see and ears to hear! Please give them a greater sense of awe and wonder. You are the God who visits Your people. Let us meet with the cloud of witnesses that hold the keys to our calling and future. Lead us in Your straight paths and open doors before all of us that only You can open and no man can close.*

Seven

Power to Produce Wealth

I will never forget a word that a man prophesied over me before my family traveled to Georgia. A year prior, the Lord told me to shut down a business I had owned and operated for more than six years. The reason was that He wanted to spend time with me. It was during that time that God freed me from more than twenty years of addiction. I soaked up God's Word and began to learn who I am in Christ.

Shortly after this happened, finances began to deplete. After a few months, I felt the season begin to shift. I wanted to work. One day as I drove home from taking our children to school, I passed by a "need help" sign at a local church. I heard the Holy Spirit tell me to apply. Within a few days, I started driving a food truck for a local food pantry. I went to specific stores to pick up donations for the pantry. I will never forget the day I overheard the word *volunteer* used in a sentence by one of the workers. At that moment, I realized it was an unpaid position. Though I did not get paid, I had God's favor. The pantry sent food home with me almost daily. However, we fell further behind on our bills. I kept asking the Lord what to do, but nothing opened up. To catch up on rent, I sold our second car. I then had to ensure that I had dropped my wife off at work and picked her up roughly an hour from home. I felt stuck.

Although we believed for a miracle, we could not pay rent again the following month. As a result, the apartment evicted us. The eviction was a tremendous disappointment because we knew that we were obeying the voice of the Lord.

We moved in with my sister, which kept us from living on the street. From a natural perspective, our circumstances did not make sense. I could not understand why following God could lead to such heartache. Looking back, I can see how God led us into our destiny. The trauma of eviction led us to a deeper trust in God. We had no choice but to wait for Him. As an update, God restored everything that we lost. We have a much more beautiful home. God gave us better resources than we had in all prior years. But more importantly, we are learning to walk by faith and not by sight.

But I remember sitting outside on my sister's porch and feeling like there seemed to be no way out financially. We did not want to be a burden. We desperately wanted a place of our own. As I sat there, I saw a spiderweb. A bug was caught on the corner and was struggling to get free. I watched the insect fighting for his life, knowing that it would soon become a meal. Suddenly, out of nowhere, a red bird flew over and clipped the web. The insect that had been fighting to get free fell to the ground. At that moment, I knew God knew what I was going through and had sent help to free us!

A short time later, we went to this little church where an anointed prophetic man was the pastor. After the service, he told me he wanted to prophesy over me. Although I had never met him before, he declared Deuteronomy 8:18 over my life. He shared that God knew that I was struggling to find a way to provide income for our family; He was going to connect the intelligence in my mind and hands to produce wealth. As I studied the verse in the months to come, I realized that God was the one who gave me the "power to produce wealth." The Greek word for power, *koach*, means the resources, drive, desire, and plans to accomplish the task. God was going to provide the way, path, method, passion, drive, and income for me to produce wealth for my family.

When I started working at a car auction in Atlanta, I began to see 818 everywhere as well as 808. Every time I saw it, I thanked God that He was providing the means and method for me to work and produce wealth. I made very little income moving cars and worked between ten and twelve hours daily. It was humbling, and it was hard to stay positive. One day at work, while meditating on Deuteronomy 8:18, God directed my attention to the first part of the verse. I was not to forget God. He was the one who would give me the power to produce wealth. As I pondered what Father was saying, it hit me. In the past, I had taken God for granted. I assumed that the favor and blessings in my life came from my hard work. I claimed responsibility for my success in a prideful way. I had forgotten the one who had given me a measure of success in my industry. After I repented and began to thank God for all of my past success and thank Him for His divine favor, God opened up a door for me. The new opportunity doubled my previous income while working fewer hours. I was able to spend more time with my Father as well as my family. As our budget increased, our life became more comfortable.

And I was not the only one who was blessed. The retail store where I started working was at the bottom of the national sales performance list. Our performance grew as a team. During my last month at that location, we found ourselves number one in the district. Do I take any glory for this? No. He is the one who gives me the power to produce wealth. I continue to see 818 to this day. He is giving me the ability to create wealth, and I continue to thank Him and give Him the glory for it.

This message goes to someone reading this book. I know that you lost your job and feel stuck. Circumstances seem very hard. You are not sure what to do for work. There appears to be a mountain or several mountains in your way. I prophesy the same to you. Deuteronomy 8:18 says, "Remember the LORD your God. He is the one who gives you power to be successful, in order to fulfill the covenant He confirmed to your ancestors with an oath." And it starts right now.

Father, I thank You for my brothers and sisters. I thank You that You are the God who provides—Jehovah-Jireh. I thank You for opening doors of provision for them. Help us remember that You are the one who gives us the power, drive, desire, resources, and plans to produce wealth. I thank You for all of the testimonies that will come as a result of what You are teaching us. Open up new ways of communication with us, like the number 818, that help us understand our season. Thank You for Your great grace and faith to believe!

Eight

Right on Time

While driving as a volunteer for a food pantry in a local church, I met a gentleman with whom I had a lot in common. He had taken many faith journeys with the Lord. One day, he told me that God was the inventor of right-on-time technologies. He shared a testimony with me that went right along with it, as he worked in the technology field. This saying has stuck with me: God is never late but not usually early. He is right on time.

As we prepared to leave Kansas City, we heard the song by Aaron Cole and Toby Mac, "His Love Is Always Right on Time." I have listened to phrases of the song in my mind many times during some of our hardest moments. The space between the provision and the promise is often the most challenging. We have God's promise, but we do not see the manifestation, at least not for a long while. Noah had the promise of rain with no storm clouds in sight. Abraham had the promise of blessed generations of ancestors before he had a single son. When we are in the most challenging times, it is easy to forget His Word and focus on the circumstances. *Right on time* would always remind me that the promise was coming, but I needed to believe what He said and not let go.

Then it happened. I started to see the number 909 everywhere. After a short time, it became apparent that God was adding to my vocabulary with Him. After seeking His face on what it meant, I heard, "Right on time."

For years, I had decided that I did not want any more children. My wife would ask me from time to time if I would be open to having more children, but my response was always no and an assortment of selfish reasons why I didn't want to have any more. One day while spending time with the Lord, about a year before we left Kansas City, I heard clearly, "You are going to have a son and are going to name him Josiah." I waited several months before sharing the word with her. She was so excited! Two different spirit-filled people prophesied a month later that we would have another child.

Several months later, I had an open vision while worshipping and praying to the Lord. I saw a high chair. I saw every detail of the chair up close. Once the vision was over, I felt that the Lord was telling me that once I saw this high chair, I would know that we were pregnant.

For over a year, every time my wife was a few days late for her monthly, we would get excited and wonder if it was time. Month after month, nothing happened. I remember my wife asking me if I was sure that we were going to have another child. After all, she was now forty years old.

I kept seeing 909. One day, the Lord directed me to Romans chapter 9. As I reached the book of Romans 9:9, I suddenly knew. The Lord told me to share with my wife that He would fulfill his promise at the "right time" or "right on time."

Anytime I see 909, He is reminding me that the promises He has made to us will happen in their proper time. It is His way of encouraging and motivating us to keep going. I do not yet understand why He showed me 909 instead of 99; however, I love how He doesn't waste anything. There are mysteries throughout scripture. There are mysteries that God invites us to enter with Him. It is a king's glory to search out and keep on seeking God's wisdom.

You may be in a difficult season, like the Israelites, between the promise of God and its fulfillment. Even though it is often the hardest, most monotonous, restless, and challenging time, you can rest assured that God will come through for you right on time.

Father, I thank You for my brothers and sisters. I thank You that You have promised that You have a destiny and a hope-filled future waiting for them. Thank You that You have promises that are all yes and amen. I thank You that You would refresh our spirits and send a new wave of hope. Remove the spirit of doubt and hopelessness. Thank You for every right-on-time promise for them. I ask that You encourage Your sons and daughters so that they will walk on into their destiny. Bless them in Jesus's mighty name!

Nine

Such a Time as This

After having a warning dream, I found myself in a situation where life was taking quick turns in a new direction. I was working sales in a smaller retail store when suddenly I was offered a full-time position in a much higher-volume store. I was going on vacation within a week and would start just as soon as I came home. I prayed about it, and my wife and I felt that God was in it. At the same time, my store manager asked me if I would be willing to join a new career-development program to become a manager. I accepted. My manager told me I needed to apply and interview for it. Because several people in the district wanted it and had been with the company longer, it was unlikely that I would be accepted this year. I filed that thought in the back of my mind. A couple of weeks later, my new store manager messaged me to ask for a picture of myself for the career-development program announcement. I was shocked and honestly a bit nervous. I never thought that it would happen that quickly.

I called my previous manager and found out that the company selected me, although I had not yet applied. For some people, that would be an exciting announcement. But for me, I was concerned about how quickly things were moving. The last thing that I want is to move ahead of God.

Three weeks later, I rode in a car to Tampa with the top sales store manager, his assistant manager, and another rep to the management training seminar. As we were talking, I found myself giving my testimony. I shared how God had set me free from lust and porn. Everyone paid attention as I shared. I could tell that several of the men were getting uneasy. One of the managers began to give excuses about how he would "look but not touch." I knew I had deposited the seeds I was there to plant. Around that time, I started to see the number 414. I was not sure why.

A week later, I shared Jesus with my assistant manager. She was a Christian but carried a secular worldview. After I finished sharing my testimony, she told me that she was glad that I had come to the store. She said that they "spiritually needed me there."

One Sunday night, I was flipping through my mostly dormant social media account and came across a post by my pastor. He had just preached a message about Queen Esther. Esther 4:14 drew my attention; "You have come to the kingdom for such a time as this."

On another occasion at work, we discussed the topic of integrity. We were talking about how we agreed that we wanted to have integrity in all of our transactions. We had heard stories of how reps would lie to customers to get a sale. I picked up my work tablet and noticed the time was 414. I instantly knew what God was saying. He sent me into the industry for such a time as this.

It does not always make sense in the natural why God has us in different places. It likely did not make sense to others why God chose to have a beautiful Jewish girl join a king's harem. But God revealed to Esther that she was there because He wanted to save the entire nation from the hand of Haman.

Working for a communications company is challenging. Working sales in wireless communications is a very cutthroat industry. I often feel like I am robbing people of their hard-earned money. One day, while spending time with God, I asked why I was in the industry. His answer was so simple. "Because I love them. They need the gospel too."

Wherever you are, God is there. He desires to reach the unreachable. He wants to flow through you to touch and light up the world through you, one person at a time. For a fire to spread, something has to get close enough to fire. You are God's fire starter. He has sent you into your mission field for such a time as this. Will you allow His fire to spread through you and touch those around you?

Here are some things to consider:

- How will your perspective of work or ministry change if you understand why you are there? Do you realize you are there "for such a time as this"?
- Are there things that God wants to change in your surroundings?
- Will you allow God to change your perspective so you can become His hands and feet everywhere you go?

Father, I thank You for placing Your children here for such a time as this. I thank You for opening up opportunities for us to reflect who You are. Show us 414 as a reminder that we are where You desire us to be. If we get off course, move us back to where You want us to be.

Ten

Persevere or Keep Going

I kept seeing the number 515. One day while driving, I asked God what it meant. He told me that he was saying that I needed to persevere. I wasn't sure why He was showing it to me. But I would soon find out.

I had just moved from a lower-volume store in Pensacola to a higher-traffic wireless store in Mary Esther, Florida. At the same time, I started the management training course. My mentor told me that my sales numbers were not allowed to slip; however, I found that I had to spend time away from the sales floor to complete the training videos. I wasn't worried because I saw 1111 multiple times and knew that God was going to provide what I needed. However, things began to pile up when my coach gave me stretch assignments. These assignments are equivalent to taking on the assistant manager role while maintaining the numbers of a focused sales rep. I was starting to feel pressure, but I knew God was with me.

Next, I found out most of the way through the first quarter of my training that I had missed a lot of study material. I felt like I was failing.

And then I was asked to begin coaching my fellow peers on their performance. This assignment was where the difficulty started.

I had just moved to this new location. It was hard for many

people to take feedback from the new guy. To make matters worse, my manager gave me the indication that she did not believe that our reps would take the coaching very well. My assistant manager told her that my training was not a priority, and if I tried to coach them, the other reps would "eat me alive." After all, several of her representatives had applied for the management training program that God had opened for me. You can see the struggle.

One day, while driving home, I began to complain to God. I felt like I was being driven in one direction by the training manager, while my store leadership pushed in the opposite direction. God would have to intervene. I began to wonder if I had missed God somehow. What if I was not in His plan? If only I had stayed at my previous location, this would not have been an issue.

After telling God I needed to hear from Him, I looked at the clock and saw 515. Tears began to flow as I heard clearly from God that He wanted me to persevere. He did not send me there to fail but to succeed. In just a week, I received feedback that changed everything. I shifted my thinking from coaching and giving feedback to looking for ways to help my teammates sell. I noticed that others started to ask me for help. Instead of focusing on my sales, I focused on the team's sales. As usual, God picked up the slack on my numbers, as customers would come in asking for what I needed sales-wise. After I discussed my leadership's concerns with my mentor, he decided to intervene and look for ways to get their buy-in for my training. Lastly, the metric I was driving was a huge success, as all of our reps hit their sales quota. God is with us and is fighting our battles for us. All that we need to do is be still and trust Him.

Here are some things to consider:

- Are you facing impossible situations?
- Because of difficulty, are you wondering what God wants you to do?

- Would it be helpful to hear a "now" word for your circumstance?
- Are you willing to allow God to speak into your situations? Will you allow Him to lead and direct you through every challenge?

Remember that challenges will fill your path as you go from glory to glory. God promises us difficulties because they allow us to grow. Every giant that you see reveals how big you are going to become when you defeat it.

By the way, I have not yet been given the scripture for this number.

Homework assignment: Ask God to reveal to you the scripture verse. If you do not hear anything immediately, do not worry. He will show you. You are His sheep. God's Word says that "He will lead us into All Truth."

> *Father, thank You for always speaking. Thank You for speaking into our challenging moments to show us that You are with us. Thank You that we can persevere because You are empowering us. Help us to keep on going even in the face of hardship. Your Word says that "we will reap if we don't quit."*

When you see 515, persevere.

Eleven

The Language of Love

> God is love.
> —1 John 4:16

God does not *have* love. He *is* love. Humanity would not have a way of understanding the concept of love if it were not for God. God does not only have love; He is the substance of love. In 1 Corinthians 12, we read, "Love is patient, love is kind …" You can substitute the word *God* for the word *love*, and it still makes sense. Why? Because God and love are synonymous.

When I asked God what to title this book, I heard *The Language of Love*. It did not seem to go together with the book. To be honest, it was tempting to scrap the title and go with something more glorious or witty until God revealed to me the purpose of the title. You see, God is love. Love wants to give. Love desires to communicate. Love is passionate about pouring itself out on others. Love has a zeal for helping.

God designed all of creation. Through sin, we fell. Humankind became selfish; humanity became consumers rather than givers. But God desires to restore His creation. It was in love that God walked with Adam in the Garden of Eden. I am sure that God shared secrets with Adam and taught him how to plant and know when to build. God poured love into humanity.

Love doesn't change. God doesn't change.

God desires to help bring complete restoration to everything that Satan, through sin, has stolen from us. God wants to help us navigate life. God has a language. His language is love.

In scripture, we see God sending angels to warn his people. Love saved the lives of those who would listen. God came to Abram and let him know about the destruction of Sodom. God loved Abram and knew that his brother-in-law was living there. Through love, God told Lot to leave and spared his life.

When the wise men were coming to see Jesus, God, in his nature (love), told the wise men of the king's evil plans to kill Jesus before He could save humanity. God spared the lives of Mary and Joseph. Love saved humanity by allowing Jesus to live until He had fulfilled righteousness at His baptism and could die according to prophecy.

Do you see it? A tyrant can command others, demanding others to listen and obey. But love is compelled to bless, help, save, and serve.

God is love. He is passionate about loving you. God will speak into every moment of your life. He will share secrets with you. Are you willing to listen?

Printed in the United States
by Baker & Taylor Publisher Services